Original title:
The Silent Elk

Author: Swan Charm
ISBN HARDBACK: 978-9908-1-0193-4
ISBN PAPERBACK: 978-9908-1-0194-1
ISBN EBOOK: 978-9908-1-0195-8

Beneath the Echoing Canopy

Beneath the echoing canopy, joy takes flight,
Colors dance in the warm golden light.
Laughter rings out like bells in the air,
As friends gather round, with smiles to share.

The scent of sweet treats wafts through the trees,
While melodies float on the gentle breeze.
Every whispered secret, and playful glance,
Spins a tale of the magic that enchants.

Candles twinkle like stars in the night,
Glowing softly, they create pure delight.
On this night, worries and cares drift away,
In the heart of this festival, we long to stay.

With every cheer, our spirits will soar,
Under the branches, we laugh and explore.
Together we'll dance, with hearts open wide,
Forever united, with joy as our guide.

Reverie in the Glen

In the glen where flowers bloom,
Laughter floats on whispers' tune.
Colors dance beneath the sun,
Joyful hearts, we come as one.

Amidst the trees, a gentle sway,
Nature's chorus bids us stay.
Glistening streams, like diamonds gleam,
In this realm, we softly dream.

Secrets of the Woodland

The woodland hides its secrets deep,
Where twilight shadows softly creep.
Underneath the arching boughs,
Magic stirs, in silence vows.

Mossy trails and rustling leaves,
Whisper tales that night weaves.
Crickets sing a lullaby,
Underneath the starry sky.

Dance of the Quiet Horns

In the meadow, horns do call,
A gentle dance to honor all.
Echoes blend, a sweet refrain,
Celebration in the rain.

Footprints trace a playful line,
As we twirl, the stars align.
With each note, our spirits rise,
Underneath the moonlit skies.

The Stillness of the Glen

In the stillness, beauty glows,
Peaceful moments, time bestows.
Here in nature's warm embrace,
We find joy, a tranquil space.

Rays of gold through branches peek,
Softly sings the woodland creek.
Gathered here, a breath we take,
In the glen, our hearts awake.

Beneath the Whispering Leaves

Beneath the leaves where laughter flows,
Joyful whispers in the breeze,
Dancing light as daylight glows,
Nature's song brings sweet heart's ease.

Children play with carefree glee,
Colorful kites against the sky,
Laughter ringing, wild and free,
In this bright world, dreams soar high.

Picnics spread on grassy hills,
Fruits and treats in bright array,
With each cheer, the spirit thrills,
Here, in this joyful, warm ballet.

As the sun begins to fade,
Flickering lights twinkle awake,
Starry magic, softly laid,
Memories made, and hearts shall break.

Den of the Hidden Herald

In the glen where shadows play,
Dancers twirl in moonlit beams,
Magic whispers, night holds sway,
Crackling fires share their dreams.

Herald calls with voice so bright,
Echoes warming hearts around,
Underneath the stars of light,
Every laugh and joy profound.

Gathered close in stories told,
Tales of love, of hopes and fears,
Embers flicker, bright and bold,
In this den, we shed our tears.

With each song, the night ignites,
In unity, we share the song,
Festive spirits, pure delights,
In this haven, we belong.

Sounds of a Shadowed Grove

Whispers float through branches high,
Harmony in nature sings,
Beneath the boughs, the voices fly,
Echoing what the daylight brings.

Children's laughter fills the air,
Bright and merry, free from care,
Every rustle, magic rare,
Life awakens everywhere.

As the day turns into night,
Lanterns glow, a warm embrace,
Fleeting shadows, soft and light,
In this grove, we find our place.

Songs of love and joy resound,
Nature's chorus, sweetly found,
Lost in wonder, all around,
In this peace, our hearts are bound.

Echoes of the Unseen

In the twilight, spirits dance,
Laughter lingers on the breeze,
Every moment, captured chance,
Whispers twirl among the trees.

Glowing orbs like fireflies,
Painting wonder in the air,
Hidden magic, soft surprise,
Enchanting hearts, a festive flair.

Stories shared around the flame,
Voices rise in joyous cheer,
Merry tales, no two the same,
Together strong, we persevere.

In the night, our hopes align,
Spirits joining, bold and free,
Under stars that brightly shine,
In this echo, you and me.

Shadows of the Ancient Ones

In the whisper of twilight's veil,
Ancient tales start to prevail.
Dancing spirits in the glow,
Echoes of laughter, soft and low.

Beneath the stars, a gathering bright,
Flickering candles, a joyful sight.
Songs of old in the air reside,
As we celebrate, side by side.

Gleaming eyes, like emeralds shine,
Together we weave, your heart and mine.
May this moment forever stay,
In the shadows where memories play.

In the Heart of Dusk

In the heart of dusk, the world ignites,
Colors burst forth, in splendid sights.
Laughter spills like a bubbling stream,
As we come alive in the evening's dream.

Fairy lights twinkle, a guiding star,
Uniting spirits from near and far.
The fragrance of joy fills the air,
Wrapping us gently in love and care.

With every heartbeat, the music swells,
Whispers of magic in ringing bells.
Hand in hand, we sway and glide,
In the heart of dusk, our hearts collide.

A Dance of Dappled Light

Underneath the canopy wide,
Dappled light dances with pride.
Nature's canvas, vibrant and free,
Crafting wonders for all to see.

Frolicking joy in each ray's embrace,
As shadows weave in a playful chase.
Children's laughter, wild and bright,
Carries the spirit of pure delight.

Every moment, a spark ignites,
We join together in festive sights.
Oh, the magic that fills the air,
In a dance of joy, beyond compare.

Reverie of the Forgotten Trails

Along the path where memories dwell,
Whispers of stories begin to swell.
In the evening's glow, we find our way,
With every step, we choose to sway.

The laughter echoes down the lane,
Woven with threads of joy and pain.
In the reverie of forgotten trails,
The spirit of festivity prevails.

Gathered round, we share our dreams,
Under the moon, where starlight gleams.
In the tapestry of night, we belong,
In the heart of joy, we sing our song.

Shadows in the Meadow

Beneath the sun's warm glow,
Laughter dances in the breeze,
Wildflowers paint the ground,
A symphony of vibrant ease.

Joyful children skipping by,
Whispers carried on the air,
Bubbles floating, laughter high,
Festive spirits everywhere.

Lanterns twinkle in the trees,
As dusk begins to gently fade,
Music swells, the heart agrees,
In the meadow, joys are made.

Stars awaken, shining bright,
Creating magic, pure delight,
In shadows deep, we find our cheer,
Together here, the end is near.

Solitude of the Antlers

In a realm where silence reigns,
Antlers high, they greet the sky,
Nature's canvas, wild domains,
Where festive whispers softly lie.

Gentle rustle, leaves' embrace,
Creatures roam with subtle grace,
Underneath the ancient trees,
Celebration feels like ease.

Moonlit paths and starlit streams,
Flickering lights, a soft allure,
A tranquil heart, in nature's dreams,
Among the antlers, we feel sure.

In this solitude, a glimmer,
Warmth within the cool night air,
Joyous spirits start to shimmer,
Festive thoughts beyond compare.

Majestic Silence

In the valley, quiet reigns,
Mountains watch with timeless pride,
Whispers echo through the plains,
As festive colors sweep the tide.

Crisp air mixed with laughter bright,
Reflecting joy from every heart,
Underneath the soft moonlight,
Togetherness is just the start.

Nature's brush paints skies so grand,
A tapestry of stars at play,
Each moment shared hand in hand,
In majestic silence, night and day.

Fleeting hours of pure embrace,
Celebration in the cosmos wide,
A festive song, we all shall trace,
In this silence, we confide.

Twilight Among Stags

As twilight drapes its velvet hue,
Stags gather beneath the trees,
Nature's ballet, wondrous view,
A festive charm in evening's breeze.

In stillness, hearts beat as one,
With every gaze, a shared delight,
Under the fading, golden sun,
Joy paints the edges of the night.

Echoes of laughter softly glide,
Through shadows cast by fading light,
Celebration flows like a tide,
In twilight's arms, we feel so right.

For in this moment, all is shared,
Among the stags, as spirits soar,
Festive breath, our souls laid bare,
In harmony, we seek for more.

Whispers of the Forest

Under the canopy, laughter flows,
Breezes dance where sunlight glows.
Leaves twinkle with a joyful cheer,
Nature sings, the heart draws near.

Branches sway with a gentle grace,
Footprints trace a secret space.
Squirrels chatter, and shadows play,
In this haven, we wish to stay.

Flowers bloom, a vibrant show,
Colors burst, and spirits grow.
Butterflies flit on soft warm air,
In the forest, magic's rare.

Beneath the sky of azure bright,
Children chase the fading light.
As dusk approaches, stars ignite,
Whispers linger, pure delight.

A Shadowed Majesty

In twilight's cloak, the pines stand tall,
Guardians silent, they watch all.
Moonlight filters, soft and clear,
In the shadows, dreams draw near.

Rustling leaves, a soft serenade,
Nature's chorus, never fade.
Owls awaken, wise and grand,
Guiding whispers across the land.

Candles flicker, a warm embrace,
Stories shared in this sacred space.
Fireflies dance in fleeting flight,
A symphony of pure delight.

The night unfolds, a gentle sigh,
Underneath the vast, bright sky.
In shadowed realms, our hearts take flight,
In majesty of quiet night.

Echoes in the Mist

Gentle whispers swirl and weave,
Misty veils that hearts believe.
Echoes hum of joy untold,
In the twilight, dreams unfold.

Softly step where echoes go,
Through the mist, our spirits flow.
Laughter lingers, sweet and light,
In the mist, all feels so right.

Wandering through a silver haze,
Time slows down in this soft maze.
Footfalls blend with nature's song,
In the mist, we all belong.

As dawn awakens, colors spill,
Heartbeat matches every thrill.
In the echoes, we find bliss,
With every moment, a stolen kiss.

Solitude Among Pines

In the woods, I find retreat,
Whispers soft, the heart's heartbeat.
Pine trees rise, a steadfast line,
In solitude, my thoughts align.

Soft needles carpet, a gentle touch,
In their shade, I feel so much.
Nature's breath, a quiet hymn,
In this peace, my worries dim.

Birdsong flutters on the breeze,
As moments linger, hearts at ease.
Each breath draws in the forest's grace,
In solitude, I find my space.

The sun dips low, a golden hue,
Casting shadows, forming new.
Among the pines, I stand and gaze,
In solitude, life's joyful maze.

Stillness in the Glade

In the glade where laughter swells,
Joyful songs, like distant bells.
Sunlight dances on the leaves,
Nature's charm, the heart believes.

Colors swirl in vibrant hues,
Gifts of warmth, the day renews.
Children's laughter fills the air,
Sprinkling joy everywhere.

Autumn's cloak, so rich and bright,
Friendships bloom in golden light.
Hand in hand, we sway and sing,
In the glade, our spirits spring.

As shadows grow and day grows late,
Memories carved, we celebrate.
The stillness wanes, but joy endures,
In the glade, our hearts are pure.

The Silent Call of Wilderness

In the wild, the whisper flows,
Nature's secrets, joy bestows.
Stars above, like gems they shine,
Guiding hearts to intertwine.

The night is bright, the moon a queen,
Dances of shadows, pure and serene.
Owls serenade with timeless grace,
Leading dreams to a sacred place.

Waves of laughter ride the breeze,
Rustling leaves in ancient trees.
Every creature joins the spree,
In this wild tapestry.

As dawn approaches, paints the sky,
We revel in the day nearby.
Nature calls, a sweet refrain,
In the wild, we break each chain.

Veil of the Antlered Spirit

In the twilight, magic's near,
Antlers crowned, the spirits cheer.
The forest hums with vibrant glee,
A veil of joy for you and me.

With every step, the ground does sigh,
Echoing laughter, reaching high.
Woodland creatures join the dance,
In this enchanted circumstance.

Moonlit paths and sparkling streams,
Whispering secrets, weaving dreams.
Antlered spirits twirl and play,
Celebrating night, welcoming day.

Each heartbeat syncs with nature's song,
A tapestry where we belong.
The veil we share, both thin and grand,
In this cherished, festive land.

Grace in the Quiet Grove

In the grove where shadows meet,
Softly lingers, a rhythmic beat.
Whispers sweet like fragrant blooms,
Filling hearts with gentle tunes.

Every leaf, a story shared,
In this grace, we are ensnared.
Among the boughs, we twirl and spin,
Finding peace where joy begins.

The sun dips low, a golden eye,
Painting dreams across the sky.
Birdsong flutters through the air,
A melody, beyond compare.

As twilight wraps its arms around,
In the grove, our joys abound.
Celebrating love, life, and cheer,
In this quiet, festive sphere.

The Enchanted Expanse

In a realm where laughter flows,
Colors dance and joy bestows,
Stars shimmer in the deep blue sky,
As dreams take flight and wander high.

Underneath a canvas bright,
Whispers twirl in twinkling light,
Each heartbeat joins the melody,
Of a world alive, a symphony.

The flowers bloom in vibrant hues,
With scents of spice and morning dew,
Children play and spirits soar,
In this realm, forevermore.

Let worries fade, let spirits rise,
As the moon casts down its sighs,
The enchanted expanse, pure delight,
Where hearts unite in soft twilight.

Secrets Tread Softly

In the hush of twilight's glow,
Where secrets tread and whispers flow,
The night unveils its hidden charms,
Every shadow gently warms.

Dancing lights flicker like fireflies,
Painting stars across the skies,
With every step, the magic blooms,
As laughter echoes through the rooms.

Underneath the velvet night,
Hearts entwined, a wondrous sight,
Beneath the trees, where secrets keep,
Festive joy, a treasure deep.

Come gather close, and hold on tight,
For in this realm, all feels right,
With every moment, memories weave,
In this dance, we all believe.

Everlasting Calm

In the heart of a gentle bay,
Where the sun greets the break of day,
Waves embrace with a soothing song,
In this place, we all belong.

Drifting clouds sail overhead,
Memories linger, joy is spread,
Children's laughter fills the air,
Every soul sheds every care.

Nature whispers soft and clear,
In the calm, we gather near,
Celebrating moments, sweet and bright,
With hearts alight in pure delight.

As the day turns into night,
Stars awaken, glowing bright,
In everlasting calm we find,
A fest of love that binds mankind.

Shadows of the Ancient Forest

In the shadows of trees so grand,
Whispers travel across the land,
Leaves rustle with secrets untold,
As tales of magic begin to unfold.

Mushrooms glow in a silvery hue,
With every step, adventure anew,
Where fairies dance in circles wide,
And dreams awaken, side by side.

The heart of the forest beats in time,
With every heart, a sacred rhyme,
Together we weave this festive night,
With laughter echoing, pure delight.

In ancient woods, our spirits soar,
Underneath the night's starry decor,
In this magic, we are entwined,
In the shadows, wonders we find.

Silence Beyond the Horizon

In a twilight glow, the world does wait,
Joyful whispers in the air create.
Stars like lanterns twinkle bright,
Guiding hearts into the night.

Laughter echoes from afar,
Underneath a silver star.
With every breath, the magic flows,
In this silence, love only grows.

A gentle breeze, a soft embrace,
Every moment filled with grace.
Together here, we dance and play,
As dreams unfold, and night turns day.

A Dance with Shadows

In the glow of the golden light,
Shadows leap, a joyful sight.
Feet that twirl on soft, dark ground,
Echoes of laughter all around.

Whirling spirits in the air,
Whispered stories, sweet and rare.
As moonlight spills on earth so bold,
Every shadow dances, uncontrolled.

Together we spin in silver hues,
Lost in dreams, we can't refuse.
Nighttime magic, hearts in bloom,
A dance that banishes all gloom.

Nature's Solitary Muse

Beneath the trees, the colors sing,
Nature's tune, a vibrant spring.
Petals flutter on warm, soft breeze,
Their gentle dance brings hearts to ease.

Scattered sunlight paints the ground,
A canvas where pure joy is found.
Every leaf, a whispered prayer,
Nature beckons us to care.

With every step, our spirits rise,
Lost in beauty, beneath wide skies.
In solitude, the world feels right,
Nature's muse, our pure delight.

Whispering Tales of the Forest

In forest deep where secrets dwell,
The whispering trees have tales to tell.
With every rustle, a story starts,
Binding together our eager hearts.

Sunbeams dancing on leaves so high,
Like a symphony beneath the sky.
Gentle streams weave a tender song,
Inviting everyone to belong.

The magic lingers in the air,
Whispers of love and stories rare.
In the forest, our spirits soar,
Forever entwined in nature's lore.

Echoes of a Gentle Past

In the warmth of golden light,
Laughter dances, hearts take flight.
Whispers of joy in the air,
Memories bloom, love everywhere.

Candles glow like stars above,
Embracing every voice with love.
Moments shared in sweet delight,
Echoes linger through the night.

Intricate Patterns of Silence

Snowflakes fall, a silent cheer,
Blanketing the earth so clear.
In the stillness, joy ignites,
Patterns woven with soft lights.

Gather round, the fire's warm,
Creating bonds that will transform.
With every glance, a story spins,
In this peace, a new life begins.

Requiem for the Forest Spirit

In the woods where shadows play,
Nature sings in bright array.
Leaves rustle with a gentle sway,
Echoing life in grand ballet.

Mossy stones and whispered trees,
A tapestry woven with ease.
Celebrating life, we unite,
Honoring all that feels delight.

Dusk's Sacred Watch

As the sun dips low and fades,
Night unfurls its velvet shades.
Stars awaken, twinkling bright,
A canvas painted in pure light.

Gathered souls in twilight's glow,
Sharing dreams with hearts aglow.
In the hush, our spirits rise,
Connected under twilight skies.

Mysteries of the Leafy Realm

In dappled light, the leaves do dance,
Whispers of magic in every glance.
Colors of autumn, so vivid and bright,
Nature's canvas, a stunning sight.

Breezes sing softly, secrets untold,
Stories of youth in shades of gold.
Branches entwined, like friends they sway,
In this leafy realm, let joy hold sway.

Creatures stir softly, a rustle of leaves,
The joy of the forest, the heart believes.
Life in the undergrowth, vibrant, alive,
In mysteries deep, the soul will thrive.

Guardians in the Underbrush

Beneath tall ferns, where shadows play,
Guardians linger at the close of day.
With eyes that shimmer, and hearts so wise,
They watch the world under evening skies.

A symphony hums, from woodlands deep,
While stars above begin to creep.
In every heartbeat, a rhythm divine,
The guardians smile, their spirits entwine.

A Quiet Reverence

In the stillness, where echoes rest,
A quiet reverence, a gentle quest.
Every flutter, a hymn from the ground,
Nature's soft chorus, a peace profound.

Moss-covered stones, like whispers of time,
Each moment lingers, each breath a rhyme.
Here in the silence, the heart finds peace,
In the reverent hush, all troubles cease.

Shadows and Starlight

Shadows stretch long in the fading light,
As starlit wonders awaken the night.
Whispers of moonbeams, tender and bright,
Celebrate magic, a festive sight.

Dance with the shadows, let laughter soar,
The night is alive, it calls us for more.
In shadows and starlight, joy intertwines,
As the world embraces these festive designs.

The Patience of the Open Field

Golden sun spills over earth's face,
Children dance, lost in their grace.
Laughter rings, a joyful sound,
In the open, life is found.

Wildflowers sway, a colorful sea,
Nature's canvas, wild and free.
Bees hum soft, a gentle hum,
In the field, hearts succumb.

Kites soar high, painted in cheer,
Every glance brings loved ones near.
Gentle breezes tell their tales,
While joy in every heart prevails.

As the sun dips, colors ignite,
Summer's warmth, pure delight.
With hope and love, the day does yield,
Embracing all in the open field.

Intrigue Among the Pines

Whispers sway in the fragrant air,
Shadowed figures, secrets to share.
Moonlight dances on bark so fine,
In the forest, truth entwines.

Echoes of footsteps, soft and light,
Mysteries bloom beneath the night.
Among the pines, a deep allure,
Curiosity feels so pure.

Stars peek through, a delicate veil,
Stories linger, faint and frail.
Fires flicker, warmth of the bold,
In the quiet, tales unfold.

Time stands still in nature's arms,
Embracing all its hidden charms.
As night deepens, the world takes flight,
In pines where hearts feel the night.

Soliloquy of the Vale

Softly flows the river's song,
Carrying dreams that drift along.
In the vale where shadows play,
Nature speaks in a gentle way.

Mountains guard, so tall and proud,
Wrapped in mist like a tender shroud.
The grasses sway, a rhythmic dance,
As if to lure the hearts entranced.

Sunbeams filter through the trees,
Birdsong rides upon the breeze.
Each moment whispers promises true,
In the vale where old feels new.

Time meanders, slow and sweet,
In every corner, joy we meet.
With every heartbeat, life keeps pace,
In the vale, we find our place.

Beauty in Stillness

Morning dew drapes the sleeping grass,
In the stillness, moments pass.
Quiet echoes of nature's breath,
Whispers of light, soft as death.

Trees stand tall, guardians wise,
Watching clouds grace the skies.
In silence blooms a secret tune,
Carried softly by the moon.

Petals unfurl with the dawn's first light,
Kissing the air, pure and bright.
In this calm, real treasures yield,
A gentle grace in the world revealed.

As evening falls, shadows blend,
In the stillness, hearts can mend.
Finding beauty in quiet places,
In stillness, love embraces.

Nature's Whispering Giants

In forests deep where sunlight beams,
The ancient trees share secret dreams.
Their rustling leaves, a soft parade,
In nature's dance, their roots cascade.

With every breeze, they sway and cheer,
A symphony that fills the ear.
The blooms awaken, colors bright,
A canvas drawn in pure delight.

Dusk's Gentle Watchers

As twilight falls, the sky ignites,
With hues of gold and soft delights.
The stars appear, a twinkling band,
While night unfolds its velvet hand.

The moon ascends, a glowing smile,
Illuminating every mile.
The night owls call, a whispered tune,
With laughter felt beneath the moon.

The Quiet Trail

Along the path where shadows play,
The sunlight dips, then fades away.
Each step reveals a story told,
Of seasons past and dreams of gold.

With every turn, the blossoms sway,
In gentle breezes' sweet ballet.
A tranquil world, serene and bright,
Invites us in to share its light.

Gaze of the Gentle Giant

High on the hill, a giant stands,
With watchful eyes and open hands.
He prompts the world to slow its pace,
And find the joy in nature's grace.

His presence warms the winter chill,
As blossoms bloom and rivers thrill.
His heart, a beacon shining clear,
Calls every soul to linger near.

Heralds of the Silent Woods

In the hush of the twilight glow,
Whispers of joy begin to flow.
Leaves dance in a gentle breeze,
Nature's laughter, pure with ease.

Banners of light twirl in the trees,
Embracing the air with playful glee.
Animals gather, hearts entwined,
In this festive moment, peace we find.

Songs of the birds, a sweet refrain,
Unity found in sun and rain.
Colors sparkle, vibrant and bright,
Heralding dreams that take flight.

As shadows lengthen, the world spins round,
Life's rhythms echo, a joyous sound.
Together we celebrate, hand in hand,
In the silent woods, we make our stand.

Solitary Majesty

On the peak where the eagles soar,
A vibrant tapestry we adore.
Mountains dressed in snow-white lace,
Whispering tales of nature's grace.

Beneath the stars, the night unfolds,
With glimmers of silver, legends told.
A solitude sweet, yet so alive,
The spirit of the wild will thrive.

Moonlight cascades on rugged stone,
Inviting us to feel less alone.
In the whispering breeze, a call to dance,
To celebrate life, to take a chance.

Each heartbeat echoes through the night,
In solitude, we find our light.
Majesty wrapped in a velvet shroud,
Within our hearts, we stand so proud.

Still Waters of the Meadow

Glistening pools reflect the sky,
Where dragonflies flit and butterflies fly.
Amidst soft grasses, laughter stirs,
In the meadow where joy occurs.

Crickets chirp a rhythmic song,
Nature's choir, where we belong.
The sun dips low, casting warm rays,
Enchanting us in golden displays.

Gathered friends under a tree,
Sharing stories, wild and free.
With every smile, the world expands,
Connected hearts and joined hands.

As evening fades into twilight's embrace,
We find our place in this gentle space.
In still waters, our dreams take flight,
In the meadow's peace, love ignites.

Silent Steps Across the Glade

Through the glade, in shadows deep,
Silent steps, a secret to keep.
A tapestry woven of green and gold,
Where stories of wonder quietly unfold.

Footfalls soft on the forest floor,
Inviting echoes, a whispered lore.
Moonlit paths where adventure calls,
Embracing tranquility, the silence enthralls.

With each breath of the cool night air,
We dance with shadows, without a care.
Beneath the arch of ancient trees,
We celebrate life with a gentle breeze.

In the stillness, our spirits rise,
Finding solace beneath starry skies.
Together we roam through nature's parade,
In silent steps across the glade.

The Unseen Majestic

In colors bright, the banners sway,
A joyful dance, a grand display.
Laughter bubbles, echoes neat,
In every corner, friends we meet.

The dusk arrives with warmth and cheer,
Whispers of joy, the night draws near.
With every spark, the stars ignite,
A tapestry of pure delight.

Fireworks bloom against the night,
Painting dreams in vibrant light.
The world spins on, with hearts so free,
In this moment, just you and me.

Songs of the past mingle with the new,
Every heartbeat, a rhythm true.
Together we raise our voices high,
As the unseen magic fills the sky.

Echoing Steps Through the Silence

Softly drifting, shadows play,
Whispers call in night's ballet.
Each step echoes, quiet hum,
In the stillness, life has come.

Moonlit paths, where secrets sigh,
Glowing trails where dreams might lie.
Every footfall, a tale unfolds,
In the silence, magic holds.

Branches sway, a gentle push,
Nature's pulse, a soothing hush.
Leaves are dancing in the breeze,
Every rustle, a whispered tease.

Hearts align with the night's soft tune,
Embracing shadows, under the moon.
In the calm, we dance our part,
Echoing steps, an artful heart.

The Still Woods' Secret

In the woods, where stillness dwells,
Nature whispers, secrets tell.
Among the trees, a dance unfolds,
In every shadow, magic holds.

Sunlight trickles through the leaves,
Memories linger, the heart believes.
Rustling laughter, a breeze so light,
Echoes of joy take flight at night.

The hidden paths where wild blooms grow,
Share their stories, soft and slow.
In stillness, we find our way,
With every heartbeat, come what may.

The woods embrace with open arms,
Binding hearts with nature's charms.
In unity, we pause and sigh,
The still woods hold the heart's reply.

Journey of the Untamed Spirit

Beneath the sky, so vast and bright,
We wander free, hearts full of light.
With every step, the world expands,
An untamed spirit understands.

Mountains call with rugged grace,
Each challenge met, we find our place.
With joy and laughter guiding us,
The journey blooms, adventurous.

Through valleys deep, and rivers wide,
Together we take each bold stride.
In every heartbeat, wild and true,
The spirit's path leads me to you.

As stars emerge in evening's glow,
We raise our hands as moments flow.
In unity, we sing this song,
The wild we cherish, where we belong.

Solace Under Celestial Canopy

Beneath the glow of stars so bright,
We gather close in joyous night.
Laughter dances in the air,
As dreams take flight, banishing care.

With every spark, a tale unfolds,
Whispers of magic, bright and bold.
The moon smiles down, a silver guide,
We share our secrets, open wide.

In this embrace, our hearts align,
Underneath the vast divine.
With every cheer, our spirits rise,
We find our place beneath the skies.

Together we sway, we laugh, we sing,
In unison, our voices ring.
A festive night, a cherished space,
In solace found, we hold our grace.

Elegy of the Hidden Wanderer

In shadows deep, a tale unfolds,
Of wanderers lost, yet heart so bold.
They tread where few may dare to roam,
A journey distant, far from home.

With every step, a whisper calls,
Through ancient woods where silence falls.
The echoes of a distant cheer,
Remind them of the ones held near.

Yet in the dark, the stars will gleam,
A guiding light, a faithful beam.
In every heart, the festive spark,
A memory bright within the dark.

So let them wander, let them seek,
For joy is found where hearts are meek.
In every moment, fleeting yet bright,
They carry the warmth of festive light.

Muffled Footfalls in Autumn's Embrace

The leaves cascade like laughter's sound,
In autumn's hold, where joys abound.
With each soft step, a tale is spun,
Of harvest moons and races run.

The air is crisp, the spice of cheer,
Reminds us all that friends are near.
In cozy nooks, with stories shared,
We toast to love, for hearts have dared.

Muffled footfalls in golden light,
As shadows play, we hold on tight.
Each moment swells with glimmers bright,
In autumn's arms, our spirits ignite.

The festive scent of cider warms,
Together we dance, the night charms.
In laughter woven, we embrace,
The magic found in this sweet place.

The Watcher at Twilight

At twilight's call, a figure stands,
With gentle heart and open hands.
The world transforms in hues so warm,
As magic weaves through every form.

A watcher waits for dreams to rise,
In painted skies, where hope lies.
Each whisper soft, a silent prayer,
For joys embraced, and burdens rare.

Beneath the stars, we gather near,
In laughter shared, we shed each fear.
The night unfolds, a tapestry bright,
In festive glow, we dance with light.

So hold this moment, sweet and dear,
For in the twilight, love draws near.
Together we sing, together we play,
As festive spirits guide our way.

Serenity Beneath the Starlit Sky

Stars twinkle bright, a joyful sight,
Laughter and music fill the night.
Fireflies dance in gentle breeze,
Hearts are light, and spirits ease.

Beneath the moon's soft, silver glow,
Friends gather close, the love will flow.
Stories shared, and dreams take flight,
Alive with joy, this magical night.

Warm hugs wrap like a cozy shawl,
In this moment, there's room for all.
Chasing shadows, feeling so free,
Under the stars, just you and me.

Whispers of love in the cool air,
Moments of peace and tender care.
Together we'll cherish the good we find,
Serenity's warmth, forever entwined.

Whispers Between the Trees

In the forest where the laughter plays,
Sunlight filters, in joyous rays.
Leaves rustle softly, a sweet, soft tune,
Nature's chorus beneath the moon.

Birds sing bright in the canopy high,
Each note a blessing, a jubilant cry.
Branches sway gently, a rhythmic dance,
Inviting us all to join in the chance.

Gathering 'round with friends so dear,
Uniting our hearts in the shimmering cheer.
Crisp autumn leaves beneath our feet,
Every step a thrill, every moment sweet.

Whispers of secrets with every sigh,
Echoing laughter beneath the sky.
In this enchanting, magical place,
We find our joy, we find our grace.

An Enigma Wrapped in Foliage

In shadows cast by a vibrant green,
Mysteries linger, yet to be seen.
Petals unfold while the daylight gleams,
Hiding secrets, whispering dreams.

Colors burst forth with a jubilant sway,
Dancing together in bright array.
Every nook holds a tale untold,
In nature's embrace, mysteries unfold.

Sunset ignites the sky aflame,
Foliage whispers, calling your name.
Curious hearts take a wander outside,
Through paths less known, let our hearts glide.

Life's enigma wrapped in lush embrace,
Finding joy in this sacred space.
With every step, let sorrows unbind,
An adventure awaits, enchanting and kind.

Beneath the Canopy's Gaze

Beneath the trees where the shadows play,
Laughter and light come out to sway.
A tapestry woven of green and gold,
Each leaf a story, each secret told.

Sunbeams dance on the forest floor,
Welcoming all who enter its door.
In this grove, every heart feels alive,
The spirit of nature begins to thrive.

Picnics spread under branches wide,
In joy and friendship, we do abide.
Moments captured in smiles and glee,
In the embrace of the grand old tree.

Together we revel, together we sing,
The beauty of life that nature can bring.
Beneath the canopy's watchful gaze,
We find our hearts lost in festive haze.

Enchantment in the Mist

Morning dew like jewels bright,
Whispers dance on soft sunlight.
Birds take flight, a joyful song,
In this dream, we all belong.

Colors twirl, they paint the sky,
Laughter echoes, spirits high.
Nature's brush, strokes bold and free,
In this moment, pure harmony.

Silent Majestic Presence

Mountains echo with a sigh,
Underneath the vast, blue sky.
Trees adorned in golden hues,
Swaying gently in the views.

Winds carry tales from afar,
Guiding dreams like a shooting star.
In the calm, we find our peace,
Silent majesty won't cease.

The Subtle Orchestra of Nature

Gentle rustle of the leaves,
Nature's song, a heart that receives.
Crickets chirp, a soothing beat,
In this rhythm, life feels complete.

Raindrops tap on thirsty ground,
In their dance, joy is found.
A melody of soft embrace,
Nature's symphony takes its place.

Veil of Midnight Woods

Stars above in velvet night,
Whispers low, the world feels right.
Moonlight spills on paths untread,
Where dreams and shadows softly spread.

Secrets linger in the air,
Each step taken, a gentle dare.
In this haven, spirits roam,
Midnight woods, a place called home.

Elegy for the Forest Guardian

In a realm where green leaves weave,
A guardian watched, firm and naive.
With laughter echoing through the trees,
He danced with the wind, wild and free.

But shadows grew as night set in,
The forest sighed, the song grew thin.
Stars above whispered soft goodbyes,
While the guardian closed his weary eyes.

Yet in the roots, his spirit stays,
In every breeze and sunlit praise.
The laughter lingers, the joy remains,
In the heart of woods, his love sustains.

So let us dance in bright moonlight,
For our guardian, who took to flight.
Through every leaf, his essence flows,
In festive cheer, our gratitude grows.

Watchers of the Whispered Woods

Beneath the boughs, the whispers twine,
Guardians gather, hearts align.
With lanterns bright, they light the way,
In the wooded dance where shadows play.

Laughter rings through the dusky air,
Joyful spirits, beyond compare.
The trees sway gently to nature's song,
As time flows swift, and we belong.

In the circle formed, stories are shared,
Of dreams fulfilled and hearts declared.
The night unfolds, a tapestry spun,
With every glance, a spark, a run.

So let the stars be our guiding light,
As we celebrate through the night.
In the whispered woods, our spirits soar,
Together we cherish, forevermore.

The Tranquil Grove

In the grove where soft winds sing,
Joyful hearts begin to spring.
Colors dance on petals bright,
Nature's canvas, pure delight.

Sunbeams filter through the leaves,
A moment captured, joy retrieves.
Laughter mingles with bird songs sweet,
In this haven, our souls meet.

Every flower, a story told,
In whispers of green, shy and bold.
The fragrance lingers, a gentle grace,
In this tranquil and sacred space.

So gather round, let spirits flow,
In the warmth of the grove, let love grow.
With every breath, we find our place,
In nature's arms, a warm embrace.

Serenade of Untold Stories

Beneath the moon's enchanting glow,
Whispers of stories begin to flow.
The air is thick with tales to share,
In melodies woven with deepest care.

From ancient roots to skies above,
Each note sings of loss and love.
The branches sway, a rhythmic dance,
Enticing us to take the chance.

Gathered 'round the fire's warm light,
We tell our tales on this festive night.
In laughter bright, sorrows shed,
In the serenade, our spirits tread.

So let the night stretch out its hands,
As each heart speaks, the joy expands.
Together in dreams, our stories weave,
A tapestry of magic, we believe.

Mysterious Hooves on Soft Earth

In twilight's dance, hooves softly tread,
Through the whispering woods, where secrets spread.
Laughter echoes, a symphony bright,
As shadows prance in the fading light.

Beneath the moon's gaze, the night awakes,
Adventurous spirits, the forest shakes.
With every step, a tale unfolds,
In the heart of the night, where magic holds.

The stars like lanterns in the sapphire sky,
Invite the dreamers to soar and fly.
In this festive realm, let worries cease,
Amidst the hooves, we find our peace.

So come, dear friends, to the woodland's heart,
Where every hoofprint is a work of art.
Together we'll weave our joyous tune,
Under the watchful eye of the moon.

Veil of the Verdant Vale

In the vale where green shadows play,
Joyful laughter greets the day.
The sunbeams dance on emerald leaves,
As nature twirls and softly breathes.

Flowers bloom in colors bright,
A tapestry woven in pure delight.
Breezes carry sweet scents from afar,
While spirits soar like the evening star.

Children's giggles echo through the trees,
As butterflies flutter on the gentle breeze.
Every nook, a place to cheer,
In the verdant vale, love draws near.

So gather your hopes, leave doubts behind,
In this lush haven, let joy unwind.
Together we'll celebrate life's refrain,
In the veil of the vale, we'll dance again.

Echoing Antlers

In the forest's heart, proud antlers rise,
Echoing whispers beneath the skies.
With each proud step, the gentle sound,
Of festive cheer in the woods abound.

Moonlit paths where shadows prance,
Invite the night to join the dance.
Voices of nature sing soft and clear,
Even the stars seem to come near.

A tapestry woven of laughter and light,
Guides lost wanderers through the night.
With antlers raised to touch the stars,
We find our joy, no matter how far.

So let the voices of olden times,
Ring through the woods in joyous rhymes.
In the echo of antlers, we find our song,
In this festive moment, we all belong.

Quiet Majesty of the Pines

In the still of night, the pines stand tall,
Whispers of wonder in their sprawl.
Beneath their boughs, the world finds peace,
In nature's embrace, all worries cease.

Branches sway with a gentle grace,
Inviting us to slow our pace.
The scent of earth and wood combines,
In the quiet majesty of the pines.

Crickets chirp a soft serenade,
As twilight cast its gentle shade.
With every breath, a soothing balm,
In this serene space, the heart is calm.

Let laughter echo from tree to tree,
In this sacred grove, we are truly free.
Together we weave our dreams anew,
In the quiet pines, under skies so blue.

Nature's Dusk Serenade

The sun dips low, painting skies,
Crimson blush, as daylight flies.
Crickets join in evening's song,
Nature's dusk, where dreams belong.

Fireflies dance in twilight's glow,
Soft winds whisper, secrets flow.
A merry hum fills the night air,
Joy and peace, beyond compare.

Birds nestle down, find their rest,
As stars emerge, nature's best.
Silhouettes in fading light,
Magical moments, pure delight.

In this realm, let hearts be free,
Festive spirits, wild and glee.
With every breath, let laughter rise,
Nature's dusk, where love complies.

A Realm Where Time Stands Still.

In a meadow where flowers bloom,
Beneath the sun, dispelling gloom.
Children laugh and run with glee,
A realm of joy, wild and free.

Butterflies float on gentle breeze,
Whispers shared among the trees.
Moments linger, sweet and vast,
In this magic, we hold fast.

Crisp lemonade by the cool stream,
Under the shade, we softly dream.
Every heartbeat syncs with the sun,
In this place, we are all one.

Time stands still, when hearts are light,
Adventures soar, spirits ignite.
Every sunset, a farewell kiss,
In this realm, we find our bliss.

Whispers in the Thicket

Among the leaves, soft voices blend,
Nature's tales, that never end.
Laughter echoes in the trees,
Whispers carried by the breeze.

Bamboo sways, a gentle dance,
Sunlight glints, a fleeting glance.
Petals fall like joyful tears,
Coloring the world with cheers.

A symphony of life unfolds,
As shimmering stories are retold.
Find magic in each rustling sound,
In this thicket, joy is found.

With every footstep in this space,
Feel the warmth of nature's embrace.
Celebration woven in each sigh,
In whispered secrets, we can fly.

Echoes of the Forest

Beneath the canopy so wide,
Whispers echo, nature's guide.
Every branch a story shares,
In the forest, joy declares.

Sunbeams glint on vibrant trails,
Breaking quiet with hearty tales.
Deer prance gently, shadows play,
In this haven, hearts sway.

Rustling leaves and distant calls,
Merry laughter slowly sprawls.
Each breath is filled with earthy cheer,
Magic lingers, ever near.

Glow of lanterns in the night,
Stars above, a wondrous sight.
In the forest, fears subside,
Echoes of life, our hearts abide.

A Symphony of Solitude

In twilight's glow, the stars arise,
A chorus hums beneath the skies.
With every note, the night ignites,
A symphony of soft delights.

The moonlight dances on the stream,
Whispering secrets in the dream.
Each breeze a quiet, merry tune,
In solitude, I find my boon.

The world outside may swirl in haste,
But here, I linger, calm and chaste.
Nature's music fills the air,
Solitude, a gift so rare.

So let the stars above me shine,
In peaceful rhythm, I entwine.
A symphony I hold so dear,
In festive silence, I find cheer.

Silence of the Ancient Woods

In the woods where shadows play,
Ancient trees sway, night and day.
Whispers echo, secrets shared,
A silent song, all hearts ensnared.

Leaves rustle softly, tales unfold,
Stories of the brave and bold.
Underneath a starlit cloak,
The forest's breath, a mystic spoke.

Mossy paths invite the feet,
In harmony, our spirits meet.
Each heartbeat's pulse, a gentle thrum,
In woods of silence, we become.

The night unfolds its velvet sigh,
Beneath the trees, we wonder why.
In festive hush, our souls entwine,
In ancient arms, the stars align.

Fauna's Gentle Serenade

In morning's light, the creatures sing,
With fluttering wings, the joy they bring.
A gentle breeze, a playful sigh,
Fauna's song, it fills the sky.

The rabbits dash with glee and grace,
While deer prance softly, keeping pace.
Squirrels chitter, a merry cheer,
In nature's concert, all draw near.

The brook hums lullabies so sweet,
With every ripple, a rhythmic beat.
In blossoms bright, the bees abound,
A serenade in nature found.

As day unfolds, the joy remains,
In every note, the heart retrains.
A festive world where life cascades,
In fauna's song, our spirit wades.

The Still Heart of Nature

In tranquil glades, the stillness breathes,
A soft embrace that gently weaves.
The tranquil hush, a velvet band,
In nature's heart, we understand.

With every rustle of the leaves,
The whispers share what nature weaves.
In tranquil ponds, reflections gleam,
The stillness holds a quiet dream.

The sky above, a canvas wide,
In pastel strokes, the stars reside.
Even the moon, so full and bright,
Poised in peace, allies the night.

So come and linger, breathe it in,
In festive joy, let life begin.
A still heart blooms eternally,
In nature's calm, we're wild and free.

Lament of the Woodland King

In the green embrace, the leaves they sway,
A crown of twigs, he roams his day.
Songs of a past in whispers flow,
Beneath the boughs where moments glow.

Echoes of laughter fill the air,
As creatures dance without a care.
His heart, a melody sweet yet sad,
For joys of youth have long been clad.

Yet in the twilight, the fires spark,
With twinkling lights in the night's dark.
Festive spirits rise like the mist,
In every shadow, a gentle tryst.

So let him reign with timeless grace,
In this enchanted, sacred space.
For even kings must bow and yield,
To the magic of the woodland field.

Serenity Beneath the Canopy

Beneath the leaves, the sunlight streams,
Creating patterns like woven dreams.
Softly the breezes hum and sigh,
As nature paints a lullaby.

The laughter of brooklets, clear and bright,
Dances through the dappled light.
Where flowers bloom in hues so rare,
And peace envelops, everywhere.

Picnics spread on blankets wide,
With friends and kin right by our side.
The joy of moments shared in bliss,
In this embrace, we find our kiss.

As stars appear in twilight's hold,
We gather tales that must be told.
A warmth ignites the evening glow,
As echoes of the day bestow.

Enigma of the Grazing Beasts

In the meadow, the shadows dance,
Creatures roam in a rhythmic trance.
With gentle grazes on emerald grass,
They weave a story as they pass.

Heartbeats synchronize with the tune,
Under the watchful eye of the moon.
Frolic and tumble in playful glee,
Universe whispers secrets, free.

The thrill of the chase, the calm of the herd,
In twilight's embrace, not a single word.
Yet every glance, a tale unfolds,
Of bonding and trust, worth more than gold.

With starlit skies, the night draws near,
Each beast and bird singing loud and clear.
A festival under the cosmic dome,
In a world so wild, they call it home.

Reflections in the Dusk

At dusk, the world begins to pause,
With painted skies, a silent applause.
Shadows lengthen, the glow ignites,
As laughter echoes through soft twilight nights.

Candles flicker in windows wide,
People gather, warmth inside.
Stories shared and hearts laid bare,
In the glow of friendships, beyond compare.

The air is filled with scents divine,
Of spices mixed in a festooned line.
From laughter's spark to music's lift,
In every moment, love's sweet gift.

As stars peek out, the night is bright,
With every glance, we find delight.
In reflection, we find our way,
In this festival, let spirits sway.

Nature's Stately Guardian

In the forest, tall and grand,
The mighty oak takes its stand.
Underneath its wide embrace,
Joyful spirits find their place.

With leaves that dance in golden light,
Whispers of the breeze take flight.
Crafted by the hands of time,
Nature's beauty, pure and prime.

Beneath its boughs, the children play,
Laughter echoes, bright as day.
A guardian through each season's turn,
In its shade, our hearts will burn.

Secrets of the Woodlands

In dappled light, the shadows creep,
Where hidden secrets softly sleep.
Among the trees, a tale unfolds,
Of ancient magic, wise and bold.

Mossy carpets, rich and green,
Nature's canvas, pure and serene.
The whispers of the leaves do sing,
Of fleeting joy and spring's bright fling.

A deer peeks out from glade's embrace,
Curious eyes in a sacred space.
With every footstep, the forest twirls,
A hush of wonder in soft swirls.

Gentle Behemoth's Lament

In twilight's glow, the giant sways,
With branches bowed in soft displays.
His sighs are heard on the gentle breeze,
A hymn of closeness among the trees.

Time has etched its lines so deep,
In mossy layers, memories sleep.
A guardian's heart, so grand, so wide,
Cradles the dreams of nature's pride.

With every fall and winter's chill,
The behemoth stands, steadfast, still.
In festive spirit, we gather near,
To celebrate what we hold dear.

Quiet Steps on Leafy Pathways

Upon the paths where sunlight gleams,
Each step unfolds a world of dreams.
With rustling leaves beneath our feet,
Joy lingers in the air, so sweet.

The forest whispers soft goodbyes,
As fluttering wings paint azure skies.
In every turn, a new delight,
Nature's beauty takes to flight.

Dappled sunlight through the trees,
In gentle breezes, hearts find ease.
Together we embark, explore,
On leafy pathways, evermore.

Guardians of the Night

Stars adorn the velvet sky,
A dance of light, they twinkle high.
The moon, a lantern in the dark,
Whispers secrets, leaves a mark.

Laughter ripples through the air,
Friends gather, casting away care.
With each jest and cheerful song,
Together, we feel we belong.

Candles flicker, shadows play,
As night unfolds, we sway and sway.
In this moment, joy takes flight,
We are the guardians of the night.

So raise a glass to all that's bright,
As we encircle fires, hearts alight.
With dance and song, our spirits soar,
In unity, forevermore.

Tranquil Whispers in the Wilderness

Underneath the ancient trees,
Softly rustles the evening breeze.
Nature wraps the world in calm,
Her gentle touch a healing balm.

Fireflies twinkle in the dusk,
Each flicker fills the heart with trust.
A symphony of nature's hum,
In the stillness, peace will come.

The mountains rise, a silent cheer,
Echoing joy, their peaks draw near.
Among the wild, our spirits roam,
In this embrace, we feel at home.

With friends beside, in soft delight,
We share our dreams beneath the night.
Each whisper heard, a magic spell,
In this wilderness, all is well.

The Hidden Majesty

Beneath the boughs of towering trees,
Lies beauty bound in nature's ease.
In secret spots where wonders hide,
The earth reveals its joyful pride.

Streams cascade with laughter bright,
Reflecting whispers of pure light.
Petals carpet the forest floor,
A vibrant tapestry to explore.

Each creature large, each creature small,
They dance around, they heed the call.
In every corner, splendor waits,
Embracing us as love creates.

Come wander here, where dreams ascend,
In hidden majesty, we blend.
The world unfolds in colors bold,
A treasure chest for hearts of gold.

Gossamer Dreams of the Woods

In the twilight, shadows weave,
Mysteries breathe, as hearts believe.
Gossamer threads of twilight glow,
Telling tales of secret flow.

Each leaf a whisper, soft and light,
Carrying dreams through the night.
With every step, the woods embrace,
A gentle hug, a warm place.

The air is sweet with fragrant blooms,
Inviting laughter to fill the glooms.
With every giggle that we share,
Together, we conquer all our care.

Under stars that brightly gleam,
We weave our lives, a vibrant dream.
In the woods, with joy we tread,
Gossamer dreams, in friendship spread.